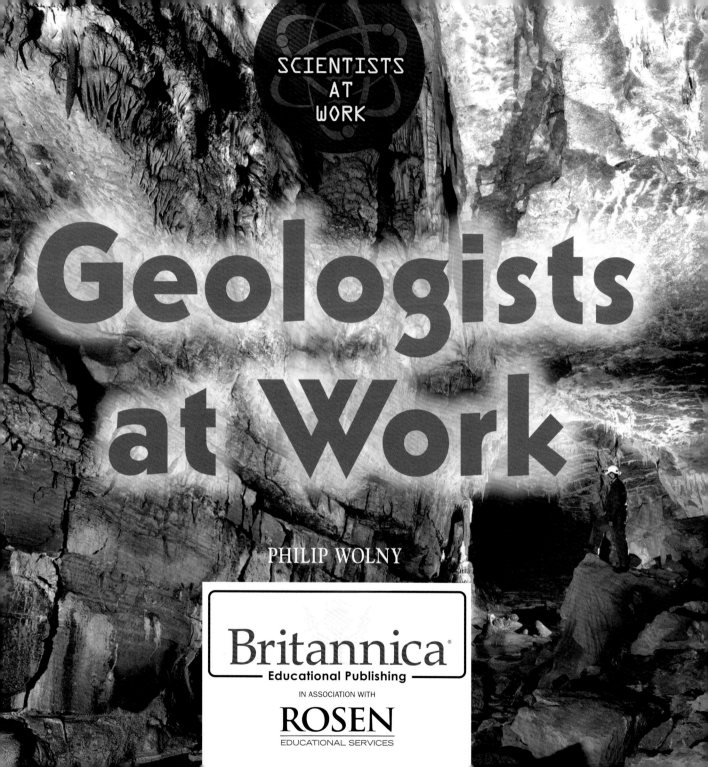

SCIENTISTS
AT
WORK

Geologists at Work

PHILIP WOLNY

Britannica®
Educational Publishing

IN ASSOCIATION WITH

ROSEN
EDUCATIONAL SERVICES

Published in 2018 by Britannica Educational Publishing (a trademark of Encyclopædia Britannica, Inc.) in association with The Rosen Publishing Group, Inc.
29 East 21st Street, New York, NY 10010

Distributed exclusively by Rosen Publishing.
To see additional Britannica Educational Publishing titles, go to rosenpublishing.com.

First Edition

Britannica Educational Publishing
J.E. Luebering: Executive Director, Core Editorial
Mary Rose McCudden: Editor, Britannica Student Encyclopedia

Rosen Publishing
Amelie von Zumbusch: Editor
Nelson Sá: Art Director
Nicole Russo-Duca: Designer
Cindy Reiman: Photography Manager
Karen Huang: Photo Researcher

Library of Congress Cataloging-in-Publication Data

Names: Wolny, Philip.
Title: Geologists at work / Philip Wolny.
Description: New York : Britannica Educational Publishing : In association with Rosen Educational Services, 2018. | Series: Scientists at work | Audience: Grades 1-4. | Includes bibliographical references and index.
Identifiers: LCCN 2016058558| ISBN 9781680487633 (library bound : alk. paper)
 | ISBN 9781680487602 (pbk. : alk. paper) | ISBN 9781680487626 (6-pack : alk. paper)
Subjects: LCSH: Geologists—Juvenile literature. | Geology—Juvenile literature. | Geology—Vocational guidance—Juvenile literature.
Classification: LCC QE29 .W65 2018 | DDC 551.023—dc23
LC record available at https://lccn.loc.gov/2016058558

Manufactured in the United States of America

Photo credits: Cover, p. 1 © iStockphoto.com/technotr; p. 4 Jon Wilson/Science Source; p. 5 Louise Gubb/Corbis Historical/Getty Images; p. 6 Courtesy of Karen Huang; p. 7 Mark A. Wilson (Department of Geology, The College of Wooster); p. 8 Microgen/Shutterstock.com; pp. 9, 10 © AP Images; p. 11 Encyclopædia Britannica, Inc.; p. 12 Konstantina Sidiropoulou/Alamy Stock Photo; p. 13 Vince Streano/Corbis Documentary/Getty Images; p. 14 Alexander Iotzov/Shutterstock.com; p. 15 NurPhoto/Getty Images; pp. 16, 19 Bloomberg/Getty Images; p. 17 ZUMA Press Inc./Alamy Stock Photo; p. 18 phdpsx/iStock/Thinkstock; p. 20 © nattapon7/Fotolia; p. 21 MCT/Tribune News Service/Getty Images; p. 22 Helen H. Richardson/Denver Post/Getty Images; p. 23 Igor Stramyk/Shutterstock.com; p. 24 © Barbara Whitney; p. 25 James L. Amos/Corbis Documentary/Getty Images; p. 26 Hawaii Volcano Observatory/U.S. Geological Survey; p. 27 Jim Sugar/Science Faction/Getty Images; p. 28 Universal Images Group/Getty Images; p. 29 dcdebs/E+/Getty Images; interior pages background © iStockphoto.com/George Clerk.

Contents

The Importance of Geologists

Geology is the study of the physical features and history of Earth. It is important because it helps us to do many things, and it answers many questions we have. How did Earth come to have its present shape and form? What are the materials in the ground, and how do they affect us? How can we use them responsibly?

Scientists who answer these questions are called geologists.

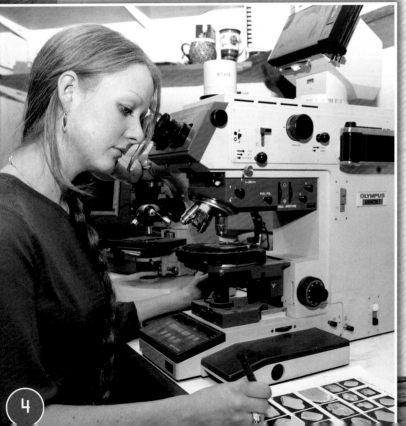

A geologist in a laboratory takes notes as she looks closely at rock samples through a high-powered microscope.

Geologists investigate a site near Lake Nyos, Cameroon, where deadly amounts of volcanic gas were released in 1986.

Geologists help find important materials in Earth's crust, such as oil, gas, and **minerals**. They also predict earthquakes and other natural hazards.

Geologists figure out where we can safely build things like houses, office towers, and power plants. They also help us save important resources, like water. Other geologists study the makeup of what is underground, including the remains of living creatures that lived long ago.

VOCABULARY

Minerals are naturally occurring substances, usually taken from the ground. They make up Earth's rocks, sands, and soils.

The Geologist's Laboratory

Most geologists agree that Earth is about 4.6 billion years old. Earth's surface has changed greatly since the planet's beginnings. After about 700 million years it developed a solid crust.

Geologists use the words geologic time to describe the vast amount of time that has passed since Earth started to form. They divide this time into three broad periods, called eons.

The Kasha-Katuwe Tent Rocks in New Mexico were formed by volcanic eruptions and by wind and water erosion into unique shapes that resemble tents or cones.

Several layers of sedimentary rock are visible at Rainbow Basin, a National Natural Landmark that is located near Barstow, California.

THINK ABOUT IT

Think about a place you know well. What changes might have occurred there over millions of years?

The two oldest eons are part of what is called Precambrian time. The third eon, which includes present time, is called the Phanerozoic eon. It is divided into three periods called eras—the Paleozoic, Mesozoic, and Cenozoic eras.

Geologists learn about these different periods by studying the many layers of rock in Earth's crust. The deepest layers are the oldest. More recent layers are closer to the surface. Each layer contains unique types of rocks and fossils.

Kinds of Geologists

There are many different branches of geology. Some geologists, such as mineralogists and petrologists, study rocks and minerals. Others study Earth's structure or investigate how landforms on Earth's surface, such as mountains, develop and change. Paleontologists are geologists who study the remains of living things they discover in the ground.

Still other geologists use geology for industry and other practical purposes. Petroleum geologists, for example, search

This paleontologist works using a special brush to remove dust and debris from the fossil of a sea creature that lived tens of millions of years ago.

for oil and help companies figure out how to extract it. Hydrogeologists study water on Earth's surface and underground. They help others decide how to use and protect it.

These are just some of the kinds of geologists. Some work in labs, and others in the field or on work sites.

Two workers for an energy company in Pennsylvania examine a map of a natural gas mine as part of their job.

COMPARE AND CONTRAST

What might be some differences between the jobs of geologists who look for oil and those who study rock samples in a lab? In what ways might these jobs be similar?

Paleontologists

Paleontology is the study of plants and animals that lived millions of years ago. It is a science that involves both geology and biology, or the study of living things. Paleontologists study fossils, which are the remains of ancient plants and creatures. Most fossils are found in the ground, in areas that once lay underwater. The ground hardened into rock over the years.

Paleontologists search for fossils all over the world. They use special tools to carefully remove fossil **specimens** from rock. They note exactly where the fossils were found. This helps them figure out how old the fossils are.

VOCABULARY

Specimens are samples collected as an example of a particular kind of thing.

This geologist is working on a dinosaur fossil at the Museum of the Rockies, in Bozeman, Montana.

LIVING RELATIONS

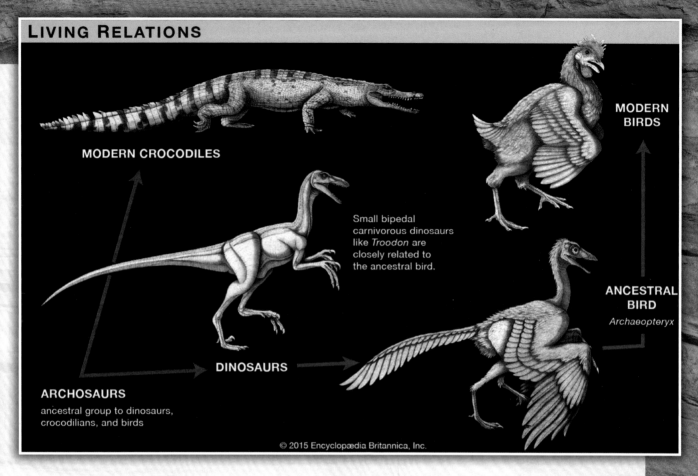

MODERN CROCODILES

MODERN BIRDS

Small bipedal carnivorous dinosaurs like *Troodon* are closely related to the ancestral bird.

ANCESTRAL BIRD
Archaeopteryx

DINOSAURS

ARCHOSAURS
ancestral group to dinosaurs, crocodilians, and birds

© 2015 Encyclopædia Britannica, Inc.

By studying fossils, paleontologists can see how prehistoric plants and animals are related to those living today. They can also tell how living things and their environments evolved, or changed over time. Paleontology can use this knowledge to create models of early forms of plants and animals, including humans.

Paleontologists help us understand how modern crocodiles and birds are related to dinosaurs.

Seismologists

Seismology is a type of geology that also involves physics, or the study of how matter, forces, and energy behave and interact. Seismologists study seismic activity, which refers to earthquakes and other vibrations within Earth and along its surface.

Lives and property depend on correct predictions of when and how powerfully seismic events will occur. When seismologists do field work, they often travel to remote, or lonely, places. This work might involve checking on machines

These seismologists are checking volcanic monitoring equipment on a tiny Greek island called Nea Kameni in the Aegean Sea.

A seismologist reads a seismograph, which records the patterns of shock waves caused by earthquakes.

that measure and record information about vibrations or movements within Earth. Such machines include seismoscopes, seismometers, and seismographs.

Information received from these devices helps geologists map Earth's inside. Patterns that geologists notice in their maps, graphs, and other readings can help them predict if or when an earthquake will happen.

THINK ABOUT IT

Seismologists are often hired to study the vibrations caused by explosions and machines used in the mining of minerals, natural gas, or oil. Why would this be important?

Engineering Geologists

A field engineer specializing in hydrogeology takes notes while testing for underground water flow.

Engineering geologists use their knowledge of geology to help figure out how and where to build structures, such as buildings, bridges, or tunnels. Long before something is planned and built, a company will make sure that engineering geologists examine the construction site.

These geologists make sure that the soil and rock beneath any project will be

COMPARE AND CONTRAST

What are some similar and different concerns that engineering geologists might have about constructing an office building and a tunnel?

safe to build on. They check to make sure that the ground is solid and safe and that it will stay that way.

Will a building remain standing after an earthquake? Will rain carry away nearby minerals and rock, making a building become unstable? Engineering geologists study a location to answer such questions. Any organization or company that builds an office building, park, housing development, bridge, or any other structure needs engineering geologists to do its work right.

Earthquakes can be very destructive to buildings that are not engineered well.

Hydrogeologists

People might not think of managing water supplies as a part of geology, but it is. Most hydrogeologists have done work in hydrology, the study of the waters on Earth's surface. Others specialize in hydrogeology, which looks at the relationship between water and the land.

Many hydrogeologists track the groundwater that exists in Earth's crust. One job that falls under this category is that of

This hydrogeologist is measuring underground water levels at a mine site in Pardoo, Western Australia.

The hydrogeologist inspecting this well works for the New Mexico Environment Department in New Mexico.

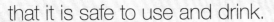

water resource manager for a county or state. A hydrogeologist in that position may test groundwater to make sure that it is safe to use and drink.

Hydrogeologists inspect wells and large underground layers of rock or sand that hold water, called aquifers. They make sure there is enough safe water for watering crops or for using in homes.

THINK ABOUT IT

Today our climate is changing and our population is growing. How important do you think hydrogeology will be in the future?

Mine Geologists

Modern society depends on a huge supply of metals and other minerals being available for our use. Without mining, we would not be able to build computers, smartphones, roads, cars, airplanes, or hundreds of other important things.

One job important to mining is that of a mine or production geologist. These scientists locate valuable minerals in a mine, pit, or **quarry**. They work closely with the engineers who handle blasting and drilling to find the cheapest and safest methods.

VOCABULARY

A **quarry** is a deep hole created by the use of explosives or by digging in order to remove rock.

Geologists help with big projects such as the Kennecott's Bingham Canyon Mine, a copper mine in Utah.

A geologist working for Century Iron Mines Corporation in Quebec, Canada, looks at a rock sample through a magnifying glass.

Mine or production geologists dig up and then study samples of rock and soil. They also lower tools underground that provide important readings and clues about the rock's physical makeup. Like seismologists, they can use these to create maps of the underground. These maps then let others pick the best places to extract materials.

Petroleum Geologists

Petroleum geologists are experts in both geology and chemistry. They use their skills to find petroleum (or oil) and natural gas, and to figure out how much probably exists in a particular place. Petroleum geologists work both on land and at sea on big platforms, called oil rigs, from which people drill beneath the ocean floor. Petroleum geologists map surface and underground areas with the help of

Some petroleum geologists work on offshore oil platforms such as this one.

Mudloggers are geologists who examine rock cuttings from wells and record their findings in reports called well logs. This mudlogger works at a mine near Pinedale, Wyoming.

photos taken by aircraft and satellites. They use devices that measure the power of an area's gravity, its seismic waves, and the chemical makeup of samples taken from underground. They put together all this information and interpret it so that drillers and others know where to drill wells and build rigs.

COMPARE AND CONTRAST

Geologists who look for oil and those who look for minerals have similar jobs. How might some of their on-the-job duties be different?

USGS Geologists

The United States Geological Survey (USGS) is a scientific agency of the US government. Many of its 10,000 workers are geologists. The USGS studies our nation's landscape and natural resources and tracks hazards like earthquakes.

One big part of the USGS's job is to map as much of the United States as possible. The special maps that the USGS makes include many topographic maps, which give information about the elevation, or height, of the mapped areas.

It once took a lot of time to map a small area. Computers and digital technology have made it much faster. USGS

This USGS geologist is marking a site to show where to take samples of earth.

Each brown line on this topographic map represents a different height. Closer lines represent a steeper slope.

geologists use three-dimensional images taken from the air with advanced cameras. Visits to the field help geologists get even more exact measurements. They do this from various points and elevations. Their work must be exact because many people rely on their information to be correct.

THINK ABOUT IT

Topographic maps exist for much of our landscape. What could be some of their most important uses?

Geothermal Geologists

Geothermal energy is heat from inside Earth. This alternative energy source can be used for cooking, bathing, and heating. It can even be converted into electricity. In some places, such as Iceland, the heat is so close to the surface it is easy to use as an energy source. In other places holes must be drilled down through rocks to reach the heat.

This geothermal power station in Iceland creates electricity from heat generated by the island's volcanic activity.

Geologists study geysers to figure out how to produce geothermal energy. This geyser is Old Faithful, in Yellowstone National Park.

VOCABULARY

Sensors are machines that respond to physical changes in their environment, like heat, light, or movement.

Geothermal geologists take rock cuttings and use **sensors** that measure conditions underground. This information helps power companies know where to drill for the heat.

Geothermal energy can help replace fossil fuels, such as oil and gas. Geologists can identify locations that have enough heat to make drilling and building a plant worthwhile. Smaller jobs might include figuring out where houses can be built to fully take advantage of heat energy.

Volcanologists

Volcanology is another exciting branch of geology. It focuses on volcanoes. Many volcanologists work in observatories. They keep track of tremors, or movements, in the earth and other signs of volcanic activity.

Other volcanologists work in the field. They visit volcanoes for an even closer look. Based on what they measure and see, they make predictions about where and when eruptions might happen. They try to

Volcanology can be both thrilling and risky. This volcanologist is taking a lava sample from a flow of Kilauea, a volcano in Hawaii.

A volcanic eruption, such as this one of Kilauea in Hawaii, is a fantastic sight for a volcanologist to witness while working in the field.

figure out how strong and destructive eruptions might be and what areas will be in the danger zone, or path of a volcanic eruption. This is important because it is difficult to get out of the path of a big eruption once it begins.

Volcanologists also visit active volcanoes to collect rock and ash samples. They analyze the effects of volcanic eruptions on the environment.

THINK ABOUT IT

Volcanologists may spend two or three months a year living in a tent near a volcano. Would a job like this appeal to you? Why or why not?

Geology Educators

A group of geology students investigates rock at Polpeor Cove in Cornwall, United Kingdom.

Another career that college graduates with geology degrees can enter is education. Some continue with their studies in geology, earning advanced degrees. They may decide to make a career of studying geology, coming up with new theories and doing field world. Instead of working for private companies, these scientist-educators work for colleges and universities. They often do original research. They report their findings in the publications that cover new discoveries about their subject, called journals.

You are never too young to start examining rocks and asking questions about them. A geology teacher will be happy to help you with your investigations.

Other geology educators want to help younger students gain a love for geology. There is a real need for good instructors to teach elementary school, middle school (or junior high), and high school students about earth sciences. Teaching is a great choice for someone who loves geology and is happy talking about it with young people.

THINK ABOUT IT

A geologist needs to be curious about Earth and its history. Do you know someone who might be interested in geology? Why do you think so?

Glossary

ALTERNATIVE ENERGY Sources of fuel that are less harmful to the environment than fuels like coal, oil, or natural gas; examples include solar, wind, and geothermal energy.

CRUST The outer part of Earth.

ELEVATION The height to which something is raised.

ENVIRONMENT All the physical surroundings on Earth, including everything living and nonliving.

FOSSIL FUEL A fuel such as oil, coal, or natural gas, formed in the ground from plant or animal remains.

GEOTHERMAL Of, relating to, or using the natural heat produced inside Earth.

GROUNDWATER Water found below the surface of Earth, especially the water that supplies wells and springs.

HAZARD A source of danger.

OIL RIG A structure above an oil well on land or in the sea that has special equipment attached to it for drilling and removing oil from the ground.

PETROLEUM A kind of oil that comes from below the ground and that is the source of gasoline and other products.

PREHISTORIC Describes something of, relating to, or existing in the time before people could write.

SEISMIC Describes something of, subject to, or caused by an earthquake or an earth vibration caused by something else.

SEISMOGRAPH A device that measures and records vibrations within Earth or along its surface.

SEISMOMETER A device that measures the actual movements of the ground.

SEISMOSCOPE An instrument for recording only the time or the fact that an earthquake occurred.

For More Information

Books

Brown, Cynthia. *Explore Rocks and Minerals!* White River Junction, VT: Nomad, 2010.

Gosman, Gillian. *What Do You Know About Rocks?* New York, NY: PowerKidsPress, 2013.

Heinrich Gray, Susan. *Geology: The Study of Rocks* (True Books: Earth Science). New York, NY: Scholastic, 2012.

Lindeen, Mary. *Investigating the Rock Cycle*. Minneapolis, MN: Lerner Classroom, 2015.

Mullins, Matt. *Geoscientist*. Ann Arbor, MI: Cherry Lake Publishing, 2013.

Oxlade, Chris. *Volcanoes* (Our Earth in Action). New York, NY: Franklin Watts, 2014.

Websites

Because of the changing nature of internet links, Rosen Publishing has developed an online list of websites related to the subject of this book. This site is updated regularly. Please use this link to access the list:

http://www.rosenlinks.com/SAW/geo

Index